The Surprise

By Heather Hammonds
Illustrations by Chantal Stewart
Photographs by Lyz Turner-Clark

T0342766

Contents

A Surprise for Tom

Jake's little brother, Tom,
was having a birthday on Sunday.

So early on Saturday morning,
Jake and Dad went to a toy shop.

Jake wanted to give Tom
a toy box.
But he didn't have enough money
to buy one. Jake felt very sad.

Then Dad had a good idea.
"I can help you to make a toy box!"
he said.

Jake and Dad went to the hardware shop.
They bought wood, nails and glue.
They bought some red and yellow paint, too.

When Jake and Dad got home,
they worked hard to make the toy box.

After the box was finished,
Jake painted it red and yellow.

"This toy box looks better
than any of the boxes in the toy shop,"
said Jake, happily.

The next day,
Jake gave the toy box to Tom.
"Happy birthday, Tom," he said.
"Dad helped me make this for you."

"Thank you, Jake," said Tom.
"This is the best toy box in the world!"

Tom's Surprise

Dear Aunty Rose,

It was Tom's birthday on Sunday.

He is now three years old.

I made Tom a toy box

for his birthday.

Dad helped me make it.

First, we went to the hardware shop.

We bought some wood, glue and nails

to make the toy box.

We bought some red and yellow paint, too.

When we got home,

we made the toy box in the garage.

Dad cut the wood for the box.

I helped him put the wood together

with the glue and nails.

Then, I painted the toy box

with the red and yellow paint.

It looked very good.

15

The next day,

Tom got a big surprise.

He said it was the best toy box

in the world!

Love from,

Jake